# FAMILY PORTRAITS

By Duane Anderson

ISBN: 978-81-19654-90-1

First Edition: 2024
Rs. 200/-

*Cyberwit.net*
HIG 45 Kaushambi Kunj, Kalindipuram
Allahabad - 211011 (U.P.) India
http://www.cyberwit.net
Tel: +(91) 9415091004
E-mail: info@cyberwit.net



Printed at Repro India Limited.

## DEDICATION

To my three families: my parents and brothers, my wife and daughter, and my daughter, her husband and their children. I love each one.

# ACKNOWLEDGEMENTS


Thanks are due to the following periodicals in whose pages these poems first appeared:

| | |
|---|---|
| Amaranth Journal | "Ice Cream Thoughts" |
| Aura Literary Arts Review | "Petals on the Floor," "Missing Person" |
| Calliope | "One Small Blessing," "Borrowed Desserts" |
| Cholla Needles | "Sunday Afternoon", "The Autumn Years of Life", "My Mother's Dancing," "Escape Artist" |
| Evening Street Review | "Where Is My Chair?" |
| Fictional Café | "Movie Days" |
| Fine Lines | "Saturday Morning Alarm," "Show and Tell," "Snow King," |
| | "Now I Lay Me Down to Sleep," "Tears of Joy, Tears of Sorrow." |
| | "Mom's Home Cooked Meals," "A Little Dust," "Reflection," "The Quiet House" |
| Freshwater Literary Journal | "Do Not Disturb," "The Big Splash" |
| Fresh Words Magazine | "The Next Moon Walk," "Climbing Mt. Everst," "Another Lesson for Dad" |
| Grey Sparrow | "Afternoon Appointment" |
| Military Experience & the Arts - As You Were: The Military Review | "D-Day Revisited" |

| | |
|---|---|
| October Hill | "Sweet Dreams" |
| Pif Magazine | "Three Hats, One Owner, Three Temporary Wearers" |
| Poetry and Covid | "Hugless Phone Calls" |
| Poetry Quarterly | "Visiting My Mother's House," "Saturday Evening Get Together," "Happy New Year" |
| Poetry Super Highway | "Am I My Mother's Husband?" |
| Rundelania | "Post-Christmas Blues" |
| Saga | "Poet's Life: Surroundings" |
| Scarlet Leaf Review | "One-Time Used Recipe" |
| Southern Quill | "Downsizing" |
| Star 82 Review | "Contagious Laugh" |
| Syncopation Literary Journal | "Wedding Dance" |
| THAT Literary Review | "Just Desserts" |
| The Good Men Project | "Charles Atlas and My Dad," "Just Another Night," "Playroom," |
| | "Before the Birth of My Daughter," "End of Childhood," |
| | "Century Celebration," "My Brothers," "Three Sons" |
| The Ibis Head Review | "Coincidence" |
| The Thieving Magpie | "Arsenic Free Water" |
| Tipton Poetry Journal | "Emergency Rooms" |

| | |
|---|---|
| Torrid Literature Journal | “612 West Thirty-first Street” |
| Cooch Behar Books | “Trouble Big Time” |

(Childhood Anthology edited by Sourav Sarkar)

| | |
|---|---|
| Cooch Behar Books | “Hey Mom,” “Visiting My Father’s Grave” |

(Father and Mother Anthology edited by Sourav Sarkar)

Ma: An Anthology of Poems in Memory of Bengali Poet Kazi Masuda Salem (Edited by Abu Zubier)
“The Mother I Know”

# Contents

# Life Cycle

Man and woman
born babies
full of holes
then left alone
to fill them in.

These are some of
the memories
filling those holes.

# First

# Family

# Poet's Life: Surroundings

A white branched sycamore
lowers its limbs as days go by
and rests its elbow against the house,
the house wakes up and scratches its beard
yes, lean on me
lean on my shoulder.

You've seen my paint, peel and chop
my boards creak
my plaster crack
and I
I've watched you grow
your leaves fall
your branches tumble
yes, lean on me
lean on my shoulder.

The tree and house still stand,
outside
a painter paints them on canvas
inside
a poet writes of his life.

## Trouble, Big Time

We are going to the linoleum store,
the linoleum store,
oh, how exciting,
that we are going to the linoleum store.

This chant wasn't anything I was singing as
I went to the linoleum store with my parents
and little brother
because, unfortunately, I wasn't old
enough to stay home by myself.
My brother and I, young and bored,
not wanting to be there, were there.

In the store, some rolls laid flat on the floor,
others, stacked,
standing straight up on their ends
like bowling pins in a bowling alley
ready to be knocked down.

Between several of the rolls standing on their ends
we saw the perfect hiding spot.
At last, our opportunity to do something while our
mom and dad talked to the salesman.
So squeezing into the opening,
the two of us hid from our parents,
to spy on others in the store.

Somehow, things did not quite work out as planned,
not that either of us had a plan.

The rolls fell like dominoes
one into another, then another,
as one of us bumped into one starting
off the chain reaction.
I thought it was my brother that set them
off into motion
and he probably thought it was me,
but no matter who did or didn't do what,
I knew it wasn't a good sign,
there was no doubt about that.

My father tried stopping
the rolls from toppling over.
If he had any success, I do not remember,
but I didn't need a fortune teller to tell us our future.
I could determine that for myself.
We were in trouble, trouble big time,
with punishment to be determined when we reached
our destination of home.

# D-Day Revisited

As a ten-year-old,
I went to see the movie **The Longest Day**
with my older brother and father
while my mother and younger brother
went to see **Old Yeller**.

This was a history lesson for me,
but for my dad,
a memory,
though he knew the outcome,
probably a painful one,
but I never knew.
I did not think to ask
nor did he say anything
that I remember fifty years later
as I watch the movie again
for who knows how many times
I had previously watched it.

## Hey Mom?

Hey Mom, won't that tree get cold without leaves?

No, it is sleeping and won't notice it.

Hey Mom, how come the sky is blue?

That is the color God made it.

Hey Mom, where is God?

God is everywhere.

Hey Mom, how can he be everywhere?

Because he is watching over every person.

Hey Mom?

# Snow King

"Hey, my son,
why didn't you finish shoveling the driveway?"
"I did, what's wrong with your eyes?"
"Nothing,
but you forgot to shovel the alley in front
of the garage.
That's part of the driveway."

"Yeah, yeah!"
Slowly I drag myself to my boots,
pull them on,
put on my jacket and gloves
and grab a shovel.

With head held high,
I walk down the sun-dried sidewalk
to the alley,
proud of my shoveling job finished earlier today,
I stop at the alley,
mumbling under my breath,
"You have to have the alley shoveled, don't you?"

Finally, I put my shovel to the cement.
Sweat flows from my forehead,
glasses steaming up,
muscles straining.

Thirty minutes later the alley cleared,
my back still good,
I walk in and salute the general.
"Ready for inspection sir."

# Charles Atlas and My Dad

I was always on the look out
for special birthday cards for my dad.
It was always fun trying to pick
out a humorous card,
the kind that always made
fun of your age no matter how old you were.
I never cared for any other kind unless
it was a blank note card with a special
handwritten note.

Anyway,
I had received an advertisement
for a book offer in the mail.
It showed a 72-year-old man,
the Charles Atlas type,
muscle bound,
for those of us old enough
to remember him.

I do not know why I received this in the mail.
Somehow, I had gotten on someone's list
as being a little older, like by thirty years.
Sometime I just feel that old
because I'm out of shape.

The ad said that you could
look like this at age 72.
I was going to send it to my dad this year
and ask him if he looked anything

like the guy in the picture,
only that my dad didn't make it to age 72.
He was short by seven months and nine days,
and I don't know if I will make it to the age of 70.
My dad's father made it to his 80's,
his grandfather made it to his 90's.
Each generation's life span seems
to get shorter and shorter.
Maybe I will only make it to 60
if the trend continues,
but it really doesn't matter
as long as I enjoy my life
like I know my father did.

He will be missed,
but not forgotten.
Happy Birthday Dad.
You would have been 72
had you lived until November.
While we are at it,
Merry Christmas and Happy New Year!

Life goes on,
but some things we always remember.

Yeah, Dad,
you didn't make it to 72,
and I miss you.

Take care
to all of us
who still remember.

# The Mother I Know

I love my mom
as most children would love their mother.
She was always around
when we were little.
Something I always took for granted
as I grew up,
not appreciating that fact until
years after I had moved away from home.

My father had a lot to do with
that decision of her staying home.
He insisted that my mom quit
working and stay home to raise
my two brothers and I.

My dad worked in the printing business,
and my mom worked at home;
cleaning, washing, fixing lunches, dinners,
breakfasts, baking.

After we were all in school
she went back to work,
first as a crossing guard, selling Avon
part time so she would be back home when
we got out of school.

Later on, when we were in junior high
and high school,
she worked full time at the same company

where my dad worked
and then took on a second full time job
taking care of the house
cooking and cleaning and all the other
things that she did before
not taking a break until way late into the night
never complaining
that I ever remember.

Oh, she didn't like us swimming in the creek
that we lived a few blocks away from,
but that never stopped us
even when we had brown blotches
on our skin from the dirty water
or the brown clothes that stunk of mud
that had to be washed.

If she complained,
I do not remember it,
even when on one of birthdays
when my friends and I
started tossing a forty pound
gunny sack full of popcorn
back and forth to each other
and the sack came open
spilling the kernels all over
the basement floor.

For some reason we left the house
and didn't help pick up the popcorn kernels
leaving that chore for my mother.
Maybe she told us to leave,
(and for good)

but I know I felt bad about that incident
and went down by the creek
and picked violets to bring
back home for my mom.
Somehow, I though those flowers
would somehow make up for all of that mess.

Whenever my mom did sit down,
maybe to read the newspaper,
it seemed as soon as she did,
her head would start nodding.
We would watch,
wondering why it didn't snap off
as it went back and forth.

Sitting down for her
was something she wasn't used to.
She never got it down pat
like I learned to do
posing on the couch
in my favorite reclining position.

For her, she always had to be busy,
and she was,
whether it was at home or church.
To my mom,
you are one hell of a woman
I am very glad I got to know.

# Years Together

On a road,
stands a couple
taking a look down the
road they've travelled,
remembering it
as if it was a short day ago.

Revisiting their world
and the years they've been together.
This road seems so close.

# Mom's Home Cooked Meals

Ah, I remember how great the meals were
as I sit in my apartment
eating some form of food that
I assembled.
The meats, potatoes and gravy,
the cakes and pies
I grew up with
were what food is supposed to taste like.
I remember these tastes well,
and what I eat now is
nothing like the memories I have
when I ate at home all those years.
Mom, get ready,
I'm coming home for Christmas.

# A Little Dust

Even on a visit, a mother
looks for dirt in your apartment,
saying there is dust on the woodwork,
the refrigerator needs defrosting.
A week later a letter is received
telling you to bring home bed spreads,
sofa covers, curtains ...

My song,
"I live in dirt,
I am filth,
come to my place
and I will let you touch it,
write your name in it.
I will remember your name
as long as the dust does not
come to bury it as all the rest."

What can I say?
My housekeeper left years ago,
and I haven't found someone else to replace her.

## My Brothers

Now that you have seen
some of the world
what part are you going to see next?
Excuse me if you think of me being nosy
but it is a closeness that I cannot part with
and I do not attempt to try to pry it away.
Not long ago I grew up with you.
Still, we are growing
but somehow, we moved to different cities.
Not that that is wrong
but there are times I must know
how you are doing.
Be patient with me
I am you brother trying to understand.

# Sunday Afternoon

A record spins on the turntable
and next side to it the leaves
from the plant move
from the winds blowing through
the screen door.

On the couch
mother sits
turning the pages of the newspaper
between the nods of her head.
Father watches the football game
on the television with his eyes closed.

Later on, we get together
and discuss a few things
over dinner
even a few jokes,
all wondering where the day went,
but not really caring to know.

# Morning Riser

Home on vacation,
rising after a night's sleep,
walking softly, hoping not
to wake anyone from their sleep,
but still curious to see if anyone
else is up and stirring.

There was someone, once,
my dad,
but he is now taking a nap
on the living room couch.
Everyone knows that it takes
a lot of energy to wake up
in the morning.
For him,
it just happened to be a little too much,
so now he is resting.

# Three Hats, One Owner, Three Temporary Wearers

A picture hangs in the living room
of my brothers, the three of us
posing with our dad.
Each of the brothers,
wearing one of our dad's hats.
We weren't just smiling,
we were laughing,
not at our dad,
but at his hats.

I look at the picture now.
Though we are all still smiling
in that picture,
I know now that
one of us is gone,
lost in a world no one knows.
It is not death,
even though we do not know it well
enough so we can understand it.
One brother hasn't found his way
out of the other world.
We are patiently waiting.
The smiles
too are waiting.

## Visiting My Mother's House

I look at the rocks lining
the bushes in front of my mother's house.
The rocks are not placed
side by side,
no, there are big gaps between each one.

I remember that summer,
digging for rocks in the creek,
lugging them back home
one or two at a time,
sometimes pulling a yard cart
with five or six rocks,
then cleaning the mud off.
I always meant to go back
for more after that summer,
but I never did.

Now, some thirty years later
I know I won't be visiting the creek again,
getting my clothes and shoes
wet and muddy
looking for pretty rocks.

I look at the gaps between the rocks
wondering why I never went back.
No answer returns,
just like years before,
no return trips.

# Three Sons

Some people are blessed
like my mother was.
She had her health
and many, many friends.

Then maybe again
she wasn't blessed.
She had three sons,
and they weren't perfect.
They caused her some trouble,
each in their own way
over the years,
but after some time passed by,
they all turned out fine.

Maybe not like a fine wine,
but at least a fine vinegar.

## The Autumn Years of Life

I took down the bird feeder
because it was harder for her to walk up
and down the basement stairs
to get the birdseed to feed them.
The birds will have to find
some other source
and the lady in the house
will have to find some other
kind of entertainment than watching them
since the birds won't return without the seed.

After almost seventy years
of singing in the choir at church
she no longer felt safe to drive
at night for choir practice
so she gave up choir.
She loved her music
and had to give part of it up.
Yes, she could still listen to it
on CDs and radio
and sing the hymns in the church with the
rest of the congregation,
but it would never be the same.

The walks outside
became fewer and shorter
with breaks in between.
Her card club called it quits
after decades of playing 500.

Time is slowing her down.
She, in her nineties,
living by herself
enjoying life
in its present form
nothing like it once was.

# My Mother's Dancing

She danced to the music
that played from the compact disc
she had just put on.
She had no partner
as she danced.

Gene Kelly and Fred Astaire were absent
as she danced solo in her family room
with no audience to watch her
or cameras to record this moment.

Did she dance like Ginger Rogers
or Vera-Ellen
in the musicals of the 1940's and 50's?

I hear about this
days later
in a letter she wrote me
and imagining me smiling as I read her words
about her dancing,
and she is correct.
I am smiling of her moment of delight.

## Show and Tell

Show and tell
was held this morning,
though little be known to me
that I was about to be
the subject to be shown.

My mother showed me off,
her son from Nebraska,
to all of her friends at church.
She was proud of her son
and I don't think I had
given her any reason not to be proud,
and I was just as proud
that she was my mother.

So there I was
being introduced again and again.
As the church service began,
I stepped off the pedestal.

# Now I Lay Me Down to Sleep

In Memoriam, Henry Johnstone
Last night I did something
that I had not done in quite some time.
I said the prayer my parents taught
my brothers and me
to say at bedtime when we were little,
though I didn't know it at the time
that they only taught us only
the first four lines out of the entire prayer,
but then, four lines is a lot easier to remember
than fourteen lines at that age.

Now I lay me down to sleep.
I pray the Lord my soul to keep.
If I should die before I wake,
I pray to God my soul to take.

I was visiting my mother years later,
and went to bed sleeping in the same bedroom
where I had slept all the years
growing up in my parent's house.
It was an old habit
that I learned years ago,
an automatic response lying in that bedroom.
It seemed strange,
but still, I was kept safe
throughout the night,
and God would have to wait for some other night.

# Am I My Mother's Husband?

The day after Thanksgiving,
a few might call it Black Friday,
but I call it hell because I was
one of the fools waiting
in one of the many long lines
with my mother loaded
with the items we wanted to purchase.
As we waited, my mother talked to various
people also waiting in hell with us,
trying, as she said, if that is possible,
to make the wait go by faster.
It didn't work for me,
but maybe it did for her.

The man she was talking to asked how long
my mother and I had been married,
thinking that we were husband and wife
rather than mother and son.

He went into mute mode,
quiet as could be,
after finding out our relationship
of mother and son,
and I started thinking,
thanks Dad,
knowing I just learned one thing from this moment,
that I have more of my father's genes than I thought,
the one that ages skin faster than a speeding bullet.

# 612 West Thirty-First Street

The time came,
but he knew it was bound to happen sometime.
The house he grew up in still existed.
It did not move anywhere,
or get destroyed by any fire or storm,
but no longer does he visit there.

He had grown,
moved away,
and over the years
returned again and again
visiting his parents,
and then came the time
when only one parent remained.

She finally sold the house
and moved out
no longer wanting to be alone,
no longer wanting the responsibility of owning a home.

He knew there would be
no more visits to this house.
Yes, the house is still standing,
but there was no one there
that he still knew.
That person had moved on
like he had done many times before.

# End of Childhood

Where am I to go tomorrow,
if I cannot stay here today?
What have I learned,
what am I to know?
Everything I thought I knew,
where has it gone?
My understanding of the world I once knew,
how did one alien thought break
through to tell me differently.
I did not wish it to happen.
Everything was fine until that one thought,
and everything else are now fond memories,
and can no longer return to it,
but in dreams and recollections.
Where am I to go?
I no longer know where home is.
I thought I was a child,
but found that was no longer the case.
I cry for my parents,
but they watch, and say nothing.
I must move on.
It is my time; my childhood has ended.

## Saturday Evening Get Togethers

We talked each Saturday evening,
mother and son, same time each week,
right after the end of her favorite television program,
The Lawrence Welk Show,

a delight to her ears, and to many others
when originally aired years ago,
and now in a second life of syndication,
a style of music still very much enjoyed.

Each Saturday, I waited until exactly 7:00 PM,
so not to interrupt one moment of her enjoyment,
and then it was our time to get together,
talking about the past week's events,

whether if it was talking about
sitting outside talking to friends,
going to an exercise class, taking a walk,
working on a jigsaw puzzle.

Yes, our lives were not quite as active
as when we were both much younger,
but our time together on the phone,
something that could not be replaced.

# On Turning Ninety-nine

My mother turned ninety-nine today,
and to celebrate, I am following the words
from the famous song:

Ninety-nine bottles of beer on the wall,
Ninety-nine bottles of beer!
Take one down,
Pass it around,
Ninety-eight bottles of beer on the wall!

It may take me sometime to finish this song
for I have something to drink between each verse
and many more candles to light on her cake,
but the celebration of my mother's birthday,
one well worth the effort.

Celebrating each year I have known her,
and all the years between my birth and her birth,
a trip down memory lane.

# Visiting My Father's Grave

I travelled three hundred miles to visit with you today.
There's no need to get up, or think
you need to speak during our time together.
If you don't mind, let me do all the talking?

I brought a chair along just in case I need to rest
my legs if they get tired from standing too long.
It has been a long time since my last visit,
and I'm not sure what I was thinking

staying away this long?
I hope this visit helps us both.
I will always be glad you were my father.
I have nothing to be ashamed of,

you have nothing to be ashamed of.
Neither of us were perfect,
but the two of us were there for each other.
I learned a lot from you and am carrying

on with the many good things you taught me.
Thanks, one more time, but before I go,
take care, until we meet again,
and the next time, it won't take me as long.

# Hugless Phone Calls

It was just another ordinary phone call, one of
those hugless phone calls where one could talk
to a loved one, but could not touch to give them a hug,

and driving for a visit wasn't an option each
time I wanted to talk to my mother,
not being a hop, skip, and jump away.

The complex where my mother lived,
finally opening their gates after being
in a coronavirus lock down mode for a year.

I made the trip for a long overdue visit,
giving her multiple hugs each day of my visit,
one to greet her, another when I left.

The hugs will come again, but for now,
I tell her I love her over the phone,
as I imagine giving her a hug one more time.

# Century Celebration

Weeks before our mother turned one hundred,
things were looking good,
the country had opened back up
after a coronavirus shutdown,
and then it returned, a bad sequel.

The facility planned for her celebration,
closed to all visitors,
friends and relatives would have to wish
her a happy birthday with cards and phone calls
instead of an in person meet and greet.

A birthday party scaled back,
only a small gathering,
the queen of the celebration,
her two sons and their wives,
the grandchildren, and great grandchildren.

Light the candles on the cake,
a cake downsized from planned.
Each candle a remembrance
of each year gone by,
celebrating all the love in her life.

# Second

# Family

# Missing Person

Two dogs wait at the top of the steps
even though there is no one on
the other side of the door.
Their friend has been gone
for a day and a half.
I know they are saying that
she should be there,
but she isn't.

They do not understand
that there has been a death
in her family.
They miss her and
she should be there.
Nothing that I do
can totally satisfy their needs.

I am not the one they miss,
but they do not know
that I miss her also,
their friend,
my friend and love.
I tell them she will be home soon.
Yes, we will be together soon.

# Reflection

Our house looks smaller
with all of our daughter's toys
scattered all over her room
and the living room.
High chairs and booster seats crowd the kitchen,
potty chair and bath toys in the bathroom
outgrown clothes and toys packed away in boxes
stored downstairs and in the garage.
Our house has become full with one little girl,
and it is not because of
all the things I just mentioned.
Her presence fills our lives,
and love for her,
and her love for us.

# I Fratelli

An hour after calling
my wife and daughter
from my hotel room
I sit in a restaurant
eating some Italian food
that I cannot pronounce.

My loneliness sets in.
I feel all alone
in this restaurant.
Sure, there are other people
sitting at the other tables
talking to one another,
but there is no one that I know
and no one sits at my table.

The ones I want here
are over a thousand miles away.
I stare into my wine glass,
lost and lonely.

# Just Desserts

My wife is craving dessert.
she asks me what we have and
I tell her orange pie,
flaming babaloo,
and cherries jubilee.

She says, no we don't,
and she is right.
We don't have anything
but a package of cookies
purchased at the store today.
Have a cookie.

Sometimes the desserts
in life are just a
plain ol' cookie.
Enjoy one before I eat the rest.

# Three Views of My Life

Daughter

Daddy, you're a good wiper.
(as I finish wiping her
after she had finished going
to the bathroom.)

**Wife**

Do you want that written on
your epitaph?
(on overhearing my daughter say
this to me.)

Me

I might as well.
At least someone will know
that I was good at something.

# Just Another Night

Last night my daughter
gave me a hug
because I told her I was through
with volleyball for another season.
She had missed me on Tuesday nights.
She told me what she wanted
to do with me,
watch her favorite show and
then play some games.

Tonight
we watched her favorite show
but we did not play a game
like she said she wanted to do.
Maybe tomorrow night
when her favorite show isn't on.

# Happy New Year

It is New Year's Eve.
My wife was tired and went to bed.
I stay up to watch
a football bowl game which has
no meaning
other than it is one of
my favorite schools to watch,
and I'm not afraid of punishment.
It might not make me happy
but I don't get depressed over it.

Between breaks in the game
I read a couple poetry chapbooks
from my library.
I might as well put part of
my mind to use.

Tomorrow I will pay for
my staying up late
like when my daughter
wakes me up at six o'clock
the next morning,
too soon
to the time I went to bed.

# Saturday Morning Alarm

Last night
my wife asked me when
I was going to wake up
in the morning.
It was a Friday night,
and I didn't have to go
to work the next morning
or get up for anything special.

How would I know?
I wake up
when I wake up.
I'm not an alarm clock
that I can set to go off
at a certain time.

Maybe I'll get up
when the paperboy tosses
the paper against the screen door.
Maybe I'll get up
when the dogs start barking
wanting to go out.
Maybe I'll get up
when it is afternoon
and the sun shines through the window,
but now since I have said this
and see you setting
the alarm clock,

I guess I'll get up at 7:00 A.M.
since that is the time you set
it for tomorrow.
So much for any further mysteries.

## Arsenic Free Water

Sunday afternoon,
I had a few seconds of boredom
as I waited for my wife and daughter
to get ready before we
went out to eat.
I was so excited by my wait
that I started reading the contents of
my daughter's bottled water.

I expected to find that
it was caffeine free
and that there were no calories
in the water,
but those statements
were nowhere to be found on the label.
Instead, the label said the water was
arsenic free,
something I always took for granted.

Someday I will read other labels,
but only if I am bored.
Right now, I'll have a sip
of my daughter's arsenic free water.
I just hope it is safe from everything else.

## Playroom

Yesterday, as I read
my daughter her nightly story,
she told me she was glad
that her bed wasn't as big as
the bed my wife and I use
because that gave her more
room for playing.

My daughter, at age six,
and me, in my forties,
our types of playing are quite different,
yet, I am quite happy
with the size of my bed
and the games
my wife and I play on it.

It is nice that
my daughter and I are both satisfied
with the size of our beds.
One small thing that is right
in this world of ours.

# Coincidence

After four days of rain
and overcast skies,
my wife asks me if I would be willing
to go back to work
cutting my vacation short.
She thinks I am a jinx,
and wants to see the sun shine again.

If I go back to work,
and even if the sun shines again,
I will not see it from where I sit.
I see only florescent lights
and the glare from my computer screen,
my sunshine and moon light.

I tell my wife no,
and it continues to rain
for the remainder of the week.
That next Monday
the rain stops,
but that is because I had run
out of vacation
the same time the sky had
run out of rain.
What a coincidence.

## The Backyard Pool

My daughter and her friend,
now both eight,
said that they would rather
play in the kiddy pool in our backyard
than go to the local city pool
where you can swim and dive
in much deeper water.

I think that they think
it would be crowded
like the slide downtown this morning,
where thirty kids arrived
all at once from the YMCA.

Sure, it might be crowded,
but we will never know.
My daughter is the lifeguard now,
complete with whistle.
Her friend, the only swimmer.
They are having fun.
What else counts?

## Before the Birth of My Daughter

Before our daughter was born
I used to canoe the Niobrara,
raft the white waters of the
Arkansas and Colorado River,
board cruise lines in the Bahamas
and Virgin Islands,
vacations in Hawaii
where I went parasailing
high in the sky above the waters,
snorkeling in the ocean,
trips to Las Vegas
where I golfed during the day
and gambled and went to the shows at night,
and when our daughter was born
I no longer do that.
Instead, I am involved
playing Chutes and Ladders,
reading Berenstain Bears books at night,
going to soccer games
or practicing with her
in the back yard,
vacations to Kansas City
visiting Oceans of Fun
and Worlds of Fun.
I am glad I had the chance
to experience these other forms of entertainment
before the birth of my daughter,
but you know what,
I wouldn't give these
new experiences up either.

## Post-Christmas Blues

My wife is in a hurry to get home.
She does not want
to stop at the Wendy's restaurant.
Instead, she pulls through the drive-thru.
She doesn't want anything to eat,
yet after we order our food,
she snacks on a candy bar and a pop.

Our daughter complains because
she has no ketchup for her chicken nuggets
and French fries.
My wife reminds her that she
asked her to check her sack
to ensure everything was there.
Our daughter grumbles again
saying she doesn't like her fries and nuggets
without ketchup,
but she eats them anyway.

I sit in the back seat eating
my chicken sandwich,
saying nothing as
we continue our trip back to Omaha.
I know now that the spirit of Christmas
has disappeared for another year.

# A Trip to the Park

My daughter and her best friend,
sliding down the long slide
at the park downtown,
sitting on paper sacks
to increase their speed
as they travel down the slides.
I watch them slide
every once in awhile
as I read the poems
from the book I brought along.
Afterwards, it is time to go the
ice cream shop to get a
Green River phosphate
or an ice cream cone.
Not much changes
from the usual ritual,
and why should it
if everything is okay with it.

# Counting

She was into counting today.
She said that she yawned fifty-one times
this morning and early afternoon.
She ate five carrots
not wanting to overdo it
by eating too many vegetables.
You bumped two parts of your body,
a knee and a wrist.
What else did you count
but did not tell me?

# Movie Days

Around Christmas time when
you were younger,
we would see the latest Christmas movie,
not that we didn't see
movies throughout the year.
We saw the three Home Alone movies,
I'll Be Home for Christmas,
Jingle All the Way,
The Santa Clause,
and The Santa Clause 2.

Back in those days
I could take you to a movie
with your friend
and sit next to you,
then things changed.
I could take you to a movie
with your friend,
but we sat on opposite
sides of the theater,
then the time came when
I could only drop you off
but I couldn't be in the theater at all,
and then,
finally came that moment
when you were old
enough to drive.
The movies changed
and our relationship changed,
not that it was bad,
but I understand.

# One-Time Used Recipe

My wife handed me a new recipe
having recently printed it from the internet,
wanting me to try fixing something different
from what we usually eat for dinner.
I went to the store
purchased all the necessary ingredients
and gave it my best attempt
in creating this masterpiece for the palate.

After dinner,
there is no mention
about liking the dish or not,
instead, complaints are heard about having to
wash so many pans, dishes, and utensils,
though it was wasn't a recipe where
one could throw everything into a crock pot,
sit back down and relax until it was finished.
Then came the complaints about the smell in the house,
that it was terrible,
even though the recipe
called for red onions and garlic.

I replied advising her
not to bother printing out any
additional mouthwatering recipes in the future.
Going forward,
we will just eat healthy frozen dinners.
The variety of meals she craves
is right there in the frozen section

at our local grocery store,
besides, using the microwave,
is something right up my alley,
and not to mention,
the cleanup and stink are minimal.

## Emergency Rooms

In the past few weeks
I have visited four hospital emergency rooms
and many doctors' lobbies
waiting and waiting
while my wife gets poked and tested

trying to find out why she is feeling the pain
that she is going through,
and EKG's, stress tests, ultrasounds, x-rays, MRIs
are parts of the new norm?
The doctors rule out certain common problems

but so far, no diagnosis
on what is causing her issues
and my wife's stress grows
until an answer has been determined,
and then what comes next?

Will it go away on its own,
is there a procedure to correct it,
will there some medicine to take
for the rest of her life?
Many doctor visits, many questions remain

in her search for an answer.
In the meantime,
I wait in another hallway with
notebook and novel
trying to pass the time as best I can.

# Ice Cream Thoughts

Inside the downstairs freezer an empty ice cream
carton sits, the container my wife emptied,
and for whatever reason, did not throw away.

Maybe she saved it as a reminder
of how wonderful the ice cream tasted,
cold, sweet with flavors of peanut butter and fudge.

Maybe she forgot, and thought it was still partially full,
looking forward to another scoop or two
of the cold treat.

Maybe the container is like a picture,
the first of many to be placed in a photo album,
a treasure for memory lane years from now.

Maybe she will tear the carton apart for another
late night snack waiting for that moment
to lick the inside of the container

still coated with the last of the remains
sticking to its sides,
making sure no portion goes to waste,

but I am just guessing.
I will just have to ask my wife
as to what is going on,

though it's not like the space
it is taking is needed to make
additional room for some other item.

## Where Is My Chair?

The rocking chair sat downstairs
in the basement,
the seat cover missing,
springs poking up,
the stain faded,
waiting to be repaired.

I took a picture of the chair
in its disrepair state,
handing it to my father
after he had retired from his job
stating it was something to keep
him busy in his retirement years.

The chair was repaired years later,
but not by my dad.
He never made an attempt, and
my mother hired someone to fix it,
and now it sits in the family room,
used at family gatherings.

And now that I too am retired,
I wonder if there is a chair in my life that
sits in some basement waiting to be repaired.
Will it receive the same result as
left by my father, or will it even be noticed?
The search begins, some day.

# Tag, You're It

Growing up, we use to play several
different kinds of tag as kids, the more
common one was as you touched someone
they were it and you were then free to run

around until you were tagged again by
the one who was it at the time, and another kind
we called freeze tag, where one had to tag
each player until everyone was tagged,

and then they were frozen in place and had
to stand still unless they were freed again by getting
touched by another player who was still untagged.
My wife and I seemed to be playing

our own version of tag this week,
not that either of us intended on playing,
our bad luck just sort of blessed us.
First, it was her turn to be it

when she went to the emergency room,
followed up with a two day stay
at the hospital, and then it was my turn to be it
two days later with an emergency surgery

followed up with an overnight stay at the hospital.
Now we are both trying to recover,
hoping to never have to play this kind of tag
again, or even hear the words 'You're It'.

# Downsizing

I

Have you ever wanted to de-clutter a room
in your home or organize your garage,
or simplify your life? Thinking about
downsizing or wondering about a living
without so much stuff? Join me for a 10-week
course on how to live a more optimal life.

II

My wife had been taking a class on Sunday mornings
on decluttering the household, and then immediately
proceeded taking on this task, after only going to
a session or two, starting first with the storage room
where boxes and boxes of decorations were stored
for various seasons and special holidays,

from autumn and winter, to Easter and Christmas,
plus other miscellaneous occasions, too many to mention.
While I, not bothering to take a class on this subject myself,
had too been going through my hoard of albums, CDs,
DVDs, books, plus a few other items over the past several
years, slowly purging them from my collection,

selling some, while donating others,
quickly finding out some things were hard to part with,
while others, like old report cards and yearbooks,
I had no problem purging myself of them.

I could have told my wife that maybe she should
have started her decluttering, beginning with her purse,

having complained from time to time that she
had trouble finding her car keys or her phone,
but I stayed quiet, fearing that I may be the one
ending up getting purged. In the meantime,
I sat in our living room eating a microwaved frozen
dinner, having gotten rid of all the pots and pans,

my dinner sitting on a TV tray, and me, sitting on a folding chair,
having already rid ourselves of most of the furniture in the house.
Soon, I can just see that there will be a for sale sign in our front yard,
for a home now too big and empty,
only to move into one of those tiny homes,
where the two of us can sit on top of each other and go insane.

# The Quiet House

Each morning there was no one to say hello to
unless I looked into the mirror and
said good morning to myself,

and on days when I ran some errands and
returned back home and parked my car in the garage,
I found the other parking spot next to mine empty.

The house was quiet, other than the furnace
turning on and off throughout the day,
or when I ran the water from the sink,

or turned on the television to watch the news,
and meals prepared each evening ended up still being
recipes for two, leaving me leftovers for the next day.

The person I missed had been gone for just a few days,
but it was as if I had lost an appendage from my body.
I kept looking, but it was nowhere to be found.

# Afternoon Appointment

I made the comment that it was almost two o'clock,
and my wife asked if I had to be somewhere.
It was true, I didn't have any meeting

scheduled with the President of the United States
for he had his own advisors and probably didn't
need any help from me, even though my opinions

were free and at least I thought they were important,
and I didn't have anything scheduled with the
local trash collector on why he didn't pick up our

garbage last week, and I'm sure he didn't want to
hear about my complaints, even if they were true.
Little did my wife remember that it was past

my usual nap time in my favorite recliner.
After all, I had to have my usual moments of
meditation, and how silly for her to forget that.

# Sweet Dreams

I wasn't up when my wife got out of bed,
a rare occurrence, for it was
my usual routine of waking up an hour
earlier, dress, eat breakfast,

read the paper, wash the dishes,
and check my emails on the computer
before she usually got out of bed and
walked into the kitchen to say good morning,

but after not seeing me up and around,
she was ready to check up on me to see if I
was still alive, but I finally woke up,
surviving another night,

living to see another day,
maybe another sunrise if it wasn't too late,
having gotten that extra rest.
Sweet dreams.

# Borrowed Desserts

She asked if she could borrow
one of my dessert cakes. Borrow,
like she was going to look at it for awhile,
a scene from the Grand Canyon,
a snow packed peak of Mt. Everest
to paint her version
of a Grandma Moses masterpiece,
then return it back,
still in its original wrapper?

It wasn't the smartest thing I've ever done,
making a loan to a relative,
even if she was my wife.
It disappeared, the ship sank,
deep into the crevice of her mouth,
down her throat, and I,
without a life preserver to rescue it.
My stomach rumbles,
another good friend, gone missing at sea.

# Third

# Family

# Tears of Joy, Tears of Sorrow

## I

## Tears of Joy - Part I

There are moments in our lives
which are so special
those tears of joy will flow
whether we want them to or not,
we seem to have no control.
In your lifetime
there have been several occurrences of these tears
showing up unexpectedly.
The first of these moments when tears flowed
happened on the day you were born,
and then again, a few days later
when we brought you home from the hospital
and laid you in your crib.
The birth of a baby,
what could be more special than that?

Since birth,
the tears of joy have flowed several more times.
The next time I remember was
you were attending kindergarten for the first time.
They flowed again as we waited in line
that first day as we dropped you off
and then the tears did not reappear until I was
sitting in my seat at the Civic Auditorium
proud as could be,
and you in your graduation cap and gown,
walking across the stage to receive your diploma.

## II
## Tears of Sorrow & Tears of Joy

After your high school graduation,
the tears changed a little,
from tears of joy
to tears of sorrow,
not that anything bad happened to you,
but things changed.

Life went on like it was meant to be.
The tears returned
as we departed the parking lot
after dropping you off at college
knowing you were no longer living at home
with us full time
and we would see less and less of you.

Tears of joy returned again, in less force,
as you graduated from college
and your internship,
but still, they showed up.
Then tears of sorrow reappeared one more time
as we left go back home
after moving you to Burlington.
We knew our home was now one less person.

## III
## Tears of Joy – Part II

And now,
your wedding day is upon us
and I know the tears will flow later today,
big time,
as I walk you down the aisle
and give you hand to your mate,
and then flow again at the reception,
where faces full of cheer and happiness will be present.

I know that this is your special day,
and you know what,
this too is very special for me.
Tears will flow
because I am so happy for the two of you,
two important people in my life,
two people I love.
My love to you both
on your wedding day.

## New Life, New Names

You were just called Baby
after months and months of being
in your mother's womb,
and now after your birth
your parents have finally chosen a name
and we can now call you something
other than Baby.

Yes, we can call you by your new name
and I guess we could still call you Baby
since you will be one for awhile
as you continue to grow,
but I like your new name
so if you don't mind
I will call you by it,
and sometime in the near future
you will also recognize it when
someone calls you by this name.

Others also received new names
as soon as you were born,
names like mom and dad,
grandma and grandpa.
Yes, your birth is the beginning of new life,
and the new names all get a second billing
because your life is what is really matters.
Welcome to a new world,
ready for exploration,
your new place on earth.

## What Will Be the First Word Said?

She is almost four months old now
gibbering like she is ready to talk
to her mother and father for the first time,
but she has yet to find the right word.
The words will eventually come.
Maybe it will be Democrat?
No, I take that back.
Maybe it will be Republican?
No, that isn't it.
She is still at the innocent stage
and hasn't been exposed to our political system yet.
Thank God for that small miracle.

And I doubt it will be words like
Supercalifragilisticexpialidocious.
Instead, it will probably be a simple one syllable word
like mom or dad or dog.
Who knows what that first word will be,
but with that first word
there will be fireworks going off
just like all the other firsts in which
are celebrated and talked about
like first time parents are known to do,
proud of their child growing up.

For myself, if I were a betting man,
I'm thinking her first word will be food,
wanting to fill her empty stomach,
but we will have to wait several months from now

until that first word is finally spoken.
In the meantime,
the gibbering will continue, and mother and father
will keep searching for that word within the gibberish.

# Contagious Laugh

Out of the blue
she started laughing out loud at her mother,
for the very first time
at the grand age of four months old.

It was a laugh that made me
want to laugh with her,
even though no one would ever know
the reason for her laughter.

It was just happened to be the right moment for her.
Maybe it was from a funny look on her mother's face.
Maybe she been holding it in
for some time and just couldn't hold it

any longer and had to release the laugher out.
Maybe she was practicing to get the
routine down right for when it
would come in handy.

Our daughter recorded this on her phone
and passed it along so grandma and grandpa
could listen to the laugh and see
the smile on their granddaughter's face.

Yes, the laugh was contagious,
making me smile in delight and wanting
to see her laugh in person the next time we visit.
Yes, she has the laugh down right.

# Moving in the Right Direction

She seemed to be bored as she
lay on her back on the floor,
and turned herself over
to lie on her stomach,
followed by rotating around
three-hundred and sixty degrees,
grabbing toys and books to keep
her entertained as she completed the circle,
but all this effort was never enough.

Time moved on and she learned how
to sit up, struggling at first to get
both feet in front of her,
and finally learning to crawl
as going around in circles
was getting her nowhere.

She is progressing along just fine
for only being six months old.
In another three months,
she will probably be tired of lying on the floor
and will be wanting to stand up and
walk like her Mom and Dad.
Yes, she's moving along,
all in the right direction.

# Walking Around

From video clips passed on from your
mother, we can see that you are beginning
to walk at eleven months, and in your

development, you are progressing along just fine.
I do not know where you are wanting
to go on your excursions in the house,

but maybe you do not want to be alone
and walk to another room to find your
mother or father, or even your dog, Ollie.

You are learning to walk, and in that process,
you are sure to get some bumps and bruises
as you occasionally fall, and take it from me,

you don't need any advice from anyone
on how to walk or take a fall, not that you
would understand any of that at your age.

You are doing quite well figuring things
out on your own as your body changes.
In the meantime, Mom and Dad will have

to continue monitoring where you walk, just
to make sure you have a safer time not knowing
anything about the dangers t

# Oh, Oh

My granddaughter came for a visit
over the weekend and taught me
a few new things like how to clean up after
she dumped a whole bowl of cottage cheese

onto the floor, causing me to think fast by
improvising with a spatula, plate and a paper
towel to clean up the mess, and while I was
cleaning up, she kept on saying, “Oh, Oh!”,

making me wonder what other mess had
she made this time, but it seemed to be her
standard response for everything she did,
no doubt something learned from her mother

and father as they too made messes of their own,
and politely used the words “Oh, Oh!”
instead of some other words that weren’t quite as
appropriate for someone only seventeen months old.

# Escape Artist

At eighteen months,
she had figured out on how to get
out of her crib on her own.
The bars no longer held her captive by
figuring out on how to climb over the rail
when she was through with her nap.
Maybe she wasn't quite as good as Houdini,
mystifying viewers as they had watched
his sensational escape acts,
but it was a start,
and she was on her way to fame,
only on a smaller scale,
first mystifying her parents.

# Bumps and Bruises

At twenty-one months, she liked running on the
sidewalk whenever she got a chance to go outside,
walking never seemed fast enough
to get to where she was going,
and it was the outdoors where she wanted to be,
no matter what the season,
rather than being contained in a room.
And though she liked to run,
her skills at that activity, though improving,
were not quite there yet, as she occasionally fell,
letting her face stop her fall instead of using
her hands to help cushion the blow,
only to sport a red nose, as if she was a clown
in the circus, and the bumps on her forehead,
worthy of a boxer causing a knock-out punch on her,
but she was a fighter, taking her bumps and bruises
with a few moments of tears to help ease the pain,
then back on her feet again, trying it all over.
One day, she may become that track star
she seems working on becoming,
but in the meantime, I just figured out
what to get her for her second birthday,
a helmet with a faceguard.

## Do Not Disturb

Our two-year-old granddaughter,
visiting my wife and I, along with her parents,
had just gone down for her afternoon nap,
after playing all morning
and finished eating her lunch,
when without fail, the doorbell rang,

waking her up, something that has now
happened on each of her last two visits.
The first time, a Boy Scout,
selling popcorn products,
and the second, a neighbor,
dropping off a sack of tomatoes from his garden.

It was then I knew I would have to invest
in a new sign, stating,
'Do Not Disturb, Baby Taking Nap',
either that, or guard the front door,
like a Special Agent protecting the President,
until the nap was finished and my job was complete.

# Eat Now

She told her dad, *Eat Now*,
but there was nothing on his plate,
nor a plate in front of him.
No food was anywhere in sight,
except what was on her tray,
and the food on there,
something not about to be shared.

The daughter,
not quite two-and-one-half years old.
Yes, Dad, eat now,
even if it is imaginary food.
Listen to what she tells you.
One who knows what she is talking about.
Just ask her.

## One Small Blessing

Fingerprints on the window,
tiny smudges appearing
after the sun's rays break
through the clouds.

The sunlight highlighting the existence
of one little girl's visit
to her grandparent's house,
a reminder of how blessed they are.

# The Big Splash

One little girl,
pink rain boots covering her feet,
wearing Minnie Mouse sweatshirt,
grey pants, and one big smile,

runs back and forth through the puddle
from last night's rain, one of the activities
in her newly found amusement park,
having the time of her life.

her own little Disney World. Splash,
Dad just got a little too close to the water,
an unintended consequence,
or one planned by this little girl,

now joining in on the fun,
resurrecting childhood memories of when
he did the same thing,
except maybe without the boots.

## Wedding Dance

The granddaughter was choregraphing
her dance moves, practicing for that day
when she would get married, a day
even she knew was years away
being only four years old, she, the great
planner, thinking way beyond her age,

and me, waiting for that time
when the wedding became reality,
especially for the dance,
one long in the making.
Dance away young future bride,
I am waiting in anticipation.

# Petals on the Floor

Fresh flowers,
just brought home from the florist
to celebrate a wedding anniversary,
but the three-year-old daughter
intercepted the flowers before
her mother got home from work,
thinking dad had brought them home for her,
picking petal after petal from each stem,
dropping them to the floor.
Was she aware of the saying
'He loves me, he loves me not'
as she picked each petal, one by one,
and discarded them to the floor?
Petals lying on the floor,
tell me the final outcome?

## Surprise! Surprise!

She called her mother after
just having an ultrasound earlier that day,
asking her if she was sitting down?

Everything was okay, well almost,
but instead of expecting one baby,
two were in her womb.

Plenty of room for a party,
as almost no one wished to be all alone,
and number one and number two joined forces.

A puzzle in the making. What would it be,
twin girls, twin boys, one of each?
No one would know until that moment when

the puzzle pieces came together, from
another ultra sound, or at the time of their birth,
but for now, their names are Baby A, and Baby B.

# Eviction Notice

At thirty-five weeks pregnant with twins,
the mother talked to the two in her womb, saying,
"If you're not out of here in two weeks,
the two of you are going to be evicted,"
having hired the enforcer, her obstetrician.

"Don't make it any tougher on me.
You have been inside me long enough.
You are healthy, getting bigger, and stronger.
I am ready to give birth,
come out, come out, enjoy a new world."

# Rock, Paper, Scissors

The time had arrived,
time to meet the rest of the world,
time to come out of mother's womb.
The one twin said to his brother,
you go first,
being quite comfortable where
he had been the past thirty-eight weeks,
but the feeling was mutual,
and his brother replied, no, you go first.

Who would be first?
They had yet to learn
the rock, paper, scissors routine
in determining that outcome.
Instead, the doctor decided,
Baby A first, followed by Baby B,
both crying as they came out,
to a strange new environment.
Welcome, young travelers, you took the first step.

## The Odd One

Dear sister,
you are the odd one.
We, your loving brothers,
were born on the same day
and you on a different day,
a different year.

You are a girl,
and we are both boys.
Yes, dear sister,
you are the odd one,
but still, we love you,
after all, we are all one family.

# Multi-tasking

Born as twins,
they were used to doing things together,
and at two months old,
they were masters at multi-tasking,
eating their meals from the bottle
as they closed their eyes as they rested,
sleeping and peeing in their diapers at the same time,
staring into space as they lay on the floor,
dreaming and sleeping,
sleeping and dreaming.
Yes, to be that age again,
and on top of it, able to multi-task.

## The Next Moon Walk

He had yet learned how to walk,
but as the music played,
he shook his head and arms,
keeping in step with the music,

ready to be the next Michael Jackson
doing his own version of the Moon Walk,
waiting for that one day when he could stand up
and show off all of his dance moves.

# Climbing Mt. Everest

He was starting out at a young age
as a mountain climber,
at the grand old age of seven months,
beginning his ascent at ground level,
on the carpeted floor
where he had been placed by his mother,
first climbing onto a cushion positioned on the floor,

then pulling himself up onto the couch,
the top of his mountain
where he planted his flag
celebrating his accomplishment,
now waiting for the next mountain to conquer,
maybe his Mt. Everest, the stairs leading to his bedroom.
His eyes light up.

# Another Lesson for Dad

Dad learned another lesson
from his son this morning.
Don't place your coffee cup
in reach of your baby
unless you want it knocked over,
spilling all over your clothes,
and burning your skin.

School was back in session,
and dad had to stay after class
to clean up the mess,
and write on the chalk board
'I will not leave hot coffee
in reach of my young son.'
one hundred times as a reminder.

www.ingramcontent.com/pod-product-compliance
Lightning Source LLC
Chambersburg PA
CBHW062111160726
48282CB00026B/751
* 9 7 8 8 1 1 9 6 5 4 9 0 1 *